ELDERCARE
IS MAKING ME
Fat

Charlotte Johnson Jones

Published by Charlotte Johnson Jones
Fredericksburg, Virginia, USA

www.charjojones.net

ISBN: 978-0-9882205-0-8

Cover design by Maria Christina Schultz

A comprehensive list of copyright, service mark, and trademark
information for intellectual property cited in this work may be found
at the conclusion.

To my remarkable husband, Herman. He surely demonstrates every day what God must desire of a caring man. And to all the adult children and their exasperating elders. Take that cupcake out of your mouth and laugh.

Contents

Chapter 1

I Sat Down on the Sofa
and I Can't Get Up

One Sunday morning about eight o'clock, I was languishing in bed, nursing a nasty head cold and stomach bug, when the ringing phone awakened me. Moments later, my husband came flying through our room on his way to the bathroom sink.

Herman splashed water on his face, slapped some toothpaste on a brush, and said frantically, "That was Mom's neighbor. She could hear Mom wailing through the wall so she called the rescue squad. The paramedics are there but they can't get into the apartment. I've gotta go help."

He charged toward the garage.

I bustled behind, asking Twenty Questions.

Did he have his cell phone? What about his

keys to his mother's place? Was she still using that burglar bar to block her door from the inside? Would anybody be able to get in through that?

How was *he* doing? At age 69, Herman has his own medical issues, which I monitor like Clara Barton. Had he had any breakfast? Had he taken his pills? Was he feeling all right? Would he call me as soon as he knew what was happening? I could come immediately if he needed me.

He drove away in a tizzy.

I collapsed and pulled the blanket back up to my chin.

Not three minutes later, the phone rang again.

It was my 96-year-old mother-in-law, fine now and calling to regale me with her latest fiasco.

She had gotten up at six o'clock and decided to take a shower, unaided. She should never attempt it but no one can stop her.

Grannie—that's what she told me to call her years ago when I tentatively tried out *Mother* on her—has reached her ripe old age through good genes, excellent health insurance, and sheer determination. Her mind is sharp but her legs are weak. Arthritis has ruined her knees and the orthopedist, wisely, will not consider replacing them. Instead, he has prescribed as much help as the law allows.

If only she would use it.

Every physical therapist, home care specialist, and aide who has come to assess Grannie's needs in the last three years has looked pleadingly at my husband or me—as though we have any influence at all—and said, "She really should have assistance when she showers. Can't you at least get her to use a bath bench?"

No.

No, we cannot.

That is why my sainted, beleaguered husband spent countless hours of his own golden years researching the best personal alert device for his mother.

He searched the Web.

He made calls.

He endured relentless sales pitches.

He reluctantly forged past Grannie's refusal to spend money on anything as superfluous as her own safety and made arrangements to install a state-of-the-art system in her apartment.

It came with a speaker box, wirelessly synced with the telephone. The box automatically connected to an operator who could talk to and hear Grannie anywhere in the apartment if the system were triggered.

The system was triggered by a pendant.

The pendant had a button Grannie could press at any time. It also contained a computer chip programmed to sense automatically if she had fallen suddenly or made an unusual move.

The whole apparatus was unobtrusive, fully waterproof, and designed to be worn 24/7.

Naturally, Grannie took it off when she stripped down to get into the tub.

And then for some reason that will forever remain a mystery, she hobbled into the living room, grasping one thing after another, hand over hand, whether sturdy enough to support her or not.

"Can't you at least get her to use her walker?" the healthcare professionals plead.

No.

No, we cannot.

In the living room, Grannie ran out of steam

and sat down to rest.

She sat down—not in the automatic lift chair that my husband had spent another precious two months of his life tracking down and having delivered—but on the loveseat.

She sat on the loveseat from which, she had remarked at least a hundred times, it is impossible to arise, even for the able-bodied.

And there she remained stuck.

I don't know precisely how close to the full centerfold she was. All I can tell you is that if I were getting ready for a shower in a slippery tub, the last thing I would remove would be that panic button.

I didn't pry, though. Maybe I didn't want to picture it. And once Grannie starts talking—especially on the telephone—it is nearly impossible to wedge a question in edgewise.

In all, Grannie said, she waited an hour or two and still she couldn't get up.

She couldn't reach the telephone.

She didn't have her pendant.

She could not even—she told me, chuckling at her own wit, while my husband, her supposedly adored son, was racing frantically across town, half-killing himself to get there—she could not even get a neighbor to respond when finally she banged on her own living room wall and started singing at the top of her lungs, "I hear you knocking, but you can't come in." She sang it for me, in full screech, through the receiver.

Except of course that the neighbor did hear, called the fire department, and called Herman. The only reason my mother-in-law was on the phone serenading me with Fats Domino now was that the paramedics had broken down the door, wrestled Grannie into a robe, and hauled her onto the chair where she should have been in the first place.

I fear this scene has been recounted in every firehouse on the Eastern Seaboard and may have gone viral. Paramedics carry cameras. I haven't had the nerve to search YouTube for "elderly half-dressed woman murders '50s tune."

Grannie, on the other hand, didn't seem to be at all embarrassed. "At least," she concluded, after she belted out her third refrain, "I made you laugh."

Honestly, at the time, she didn't.

All I could think about was whether Herman had wrapped the car around a tree trying to rescue

Grannie from her umpteenth unnecessary disaster. I was sick. I was worried. I was angry that often he is the one who pays the price for her obstinacy.

That morning, if I hadn't been laid low by a clogged head and killer virus, I would have gone in the kitchen and eaten every cookie, buttery snack, and piece of chocolate I could get my trembling hands on just to keep me from running across town myself and wringing her stubborn neck.

There, I said it.

Eldercare is making me bitchy, mean, and fat.

I wasn't even amused when I shared this tale with the few people I trust not to be shocked at my distemper. The people who will still love me no matter what. The people who will visit me in prison after I am convicted.

I could have used a sympathetic shoulder.

They didn't care.

They laughed.

They howled.

"You have got to write a book," said my stepson.

"Do it. Please do it," said a fellow writer, appealing to altruism. "Somewhere, someone needs to know that they are not the only one."

Woot. Here it is.

These stories about Grannie and my own 91-year-old mother are true. You can make this stuff up, but in our marriage you don't have to. And if a bleating undertone of utter aggravation comes through, well, believe me, that too is real.

My friend the writer is probably on to something. Anybody up to their hips in eldercare, as my husband and I have been now for far more than a decade, will tell you that it is never as easy as the Hallmark Channel makes it look.

When I see that dimpled white-haired woman in the TV commercial who sweetly acknowledges that she resisted help until the daughter actress at her side convinced her a panic button was all for the best, I just want to throw a shoe at the flat screen.

The Mothers, as we call them when Herman and I are at our most exasperated, don't have a white hair between them, although we ourselves are turning snowy faster than Marie Antoinette. Grannie keeps her hair dyed chestnut brown in an attempt to have her cake and eat it too. She likes to maintain the illusion that she is still merely middle-aged while claiming center stage for being nearly 100. Mother has a natural steely platinum bob that perfectly complements her indomitable temperament.

Both possess iron wills and could—and would—cheerfully crush the Rock of Gibraltar if it suited them.

Neither is ever misguided or wrong.

Never.

Ever.

Ask them.

The motto on their freak flag?

"You're just too sensitive. Besides, I'm your mother. I know what I'm doing."

Sound familiar? You must have an aging parent or grandparent who is driving you to the doughnuts even as you struggle to keep her well, safe, and reasonably content. You do everything in your power, and yet, it is not enough.

If misery loves company, then please read on. You won't believe the one about Mother and her underpants.

Chapter 2

I'm Glad I Had on Underpants

Let's be candid. The same sweet, white-haired woman on the TV commercial whose daughter gently persuaded her to get a monitoring system is probably wearing padded underpants, but nobody is talking.

Until very recently the only people who dared to speak the name of adult wetness control products in public were standup comics. None of their jokes would have worked if we all chatted over cocktails about which Depend style is our personal favorite.

Lately though, I have noticed that the company itself is starting to advertise its latest panty-like design on the nightly news, or on something that I watch, I'm not sure what. Maybe the *Real Housewives of Assisted Living*.

One Depend ad features a confident woman

swinging down the street. She is going somewhere interesting, dressed in sleek clothing, and not a bit concerned about sneezing violently and having to run home to change her pantsuit.

She's covered.

My mother, on the other hand, is not. On bad days, she has even taken to going totally commando through the halls of her own assisted living residence, airing it all out under her flower print skirt.

This is a recent development and was news to me because one of the challenges of eldercare is that I am always a step behind. *Always.*

I will become aware that Mother is having some sort of problem. While I am focused feverishly on a solution, she moves on to an entirely different issue.

I live four hours away, and I rely on her facility's staff, a hired visiting aide, phone calls, and my own necessarily infrequent trips to keep me up-to-date on Mother's status. It might be easier if Mother were right under my nose but it just didn't work out that way.

Thirteen years ago, I was in Kentucky

working on my mid-life crisis and a late master's degree. The very same day that I took my last grad school exam, Mother fell at her home in North Carolina and snapped a femur, or as it is known in the circles in which I travel, "She broke her first hip."

I had been keenly anticipating a two-week Christmas break before beginning a temporary job in my new field on January 2, 2000.

But instead of reading romance novels with no educational value, laying in caches of Sterno and canned goods for any possible Y2K catastrophe, and celebrating the Millennium New Year, I immediately flew to Mother's side at the hospital where she had undergone hip-joint-replacement surgery.

Staying alone at night in her townhouse, the smaller home she had purchased after my father's death fifteen years before, I realized what a predicament she was in.

Her bills were piled by the stovetop, as likely to go up in blazes as to get paid.

She wasn't cleaning anymore and it took a professional crew of four workers an entire afternoon to scour the kitchen, scrub the bathrooms, and get the grunge off the windows, windowsills, doors, floors, and baseboards.

A greasy spot on the loveseat in front of the TV matched the twin splotch on the back of the blouse that it appeared Mother wore without a break. For some time I had known that although she got the usual array of dozens of cable channels, she watched only CNN. Now I realized that was all she did. All day. Every day.

The most alarming discovery was that I found pill bottles everywhere.

In the pantry.

In the medicine cabinet.

On the counters.

Mother had duplicate prescriptions for strong painkillers and anxiety medications from different doctors and various pharmacies. She had *three* for vertigo. For months, whenever we had talked on the phone, she had complained to me about dizziness. I had a hunch she was overmedicated but every time I had suggested taking everything to her primary doctor to sort out, she had balked.

Clearly, I was not going to be able to leave her to her own devices anymore.

Normally, a parent who needs help moves closer to one of her children. As an only child, that would have been me.

Unfortunately, Herman and I were both looking for permanent jobs somewhere on the East Coast. Nothing was settled. We couldn't uproot Mother under such uncertain terms.

She refused to budge anyway.

So she stayed in North Carolina, and I reluctantly became her Long Distance Care Manager, marshalling her through years of changes and moves that eventually found her still hours away from me, still in North Carolina, but now in assisted living.

And that is why I did not know until I visited Mother not too long ago that although she needed them, for some reason she had stopped wearing Poise pads.

If you don't know what I am talking about, to put it as delicately as possible, in fact, to put it just as the company puts it on its own Web page, Poise "offers proven protection for frequent unexpected wetness."

This does not mean sudden thunderstorms.

When I realized what was going on, I was almost as awash in confusion as Mother. Up until that point, she had been handling her personal plumbing needs eccentrically but well enough.

She had never trusted the staff to wash her delicates. She was convinced that they would mix things up. That particular belief may have been my fault. Mother is so bamboozled by variations in her routine and surroundings that she clings to the known until it is threadbare and unworkable. Which, I am sad to say, describes her panties.

I think she got nervous about letting the staff get their hands on her unmentionables because I once slipped a pile of new ones in her dresser drawer in the hope she would simply begin wearing them. Instead, she thought another resident's things had been delivered to her room by mistake. As a result, she was in the entrenched habit of alternating two pair, rinsing one at night, and wearing the other the next morning.

When I arrived at her room for that recent visit, I knew something was awry when I encountered six pairs of undies—two ragged ones and four from the dresser—hanging, damp, from the

15

grab bar by the shower. On the bathroom floor sat a half-empty package of Poise covered in talcum powder.

Up to that point, Poise had been one of the things that Mother was adamant about having on hand at all times, along with easy crossword puzzle books, lipstick, and the powder, which she shakes around so lavishly that it flies in the air and settles like volcanic ash on everything.

"Aren't you wearing these anymore?" I asked, pointing to the Poise.

"No," she said. "I don't need them."

I didn't believe it.

I am no Sherlock Holmes, but if by three o'clock in the afternoon she already had rinsed out all the panties that she is willing to claim as hers, then it seems elementary that there's some "frequent unexpected wetness" going on.

And we were going out to Mother's favorite restaurant, Red Lobster, for dinner any minute.

I tried.

I really did.

I tried to get her to wear one of the other new pairs in the dresser. They were pink and they were

16

black, the rejects from a couple of assorted three-packs I once had bought at Walmart in desperation. Even at the time, I knew these were garish and forbidden colors that had never graced Mother's well-bred posterior. It was now clear they never would, even in an emergency.

I offered the driest of the pairs dangling from the grab bar, but Mother pronounced them too damp to wear. "I'm fine," she said. "I don't need underwear."

I'm pretty sure I rolled my eyes, even though I always try to be respectful.

I didn't know what to do. I didn't want to disappoint her. I didn't want to argue with her. So off we went, hoping for the best.

Thanks to a pit stop on the way *in* the restaurant and another on the way *out*, things seemed to be going swimmingly, so to speak. Then just as I was escorting Mother back toward the entrance of the assisted living building, I noticed a puddle on the sidewalk right beneath her feet. It looked an awful lot like "frequent unexpected wetness" from where I stood, which I am not ashamed to say was as far off to the side as I could manage and still open the door.

I went home and went into action. I had a strategy meeting by phone with the director of the facility and with the aide who most often works with Mother. My job was to find ultra-absorbent cloth panties lacy and refined enough to surreptitiously exchange for Mother's.

This was a variation on the plan that the director said works with residents who don't want to admit that they are losing control. Remove the old underwear. Put disposable adult pull-ups in their place. The recipient may not like it, but nobody— except for Mother—will actually go without.

I searched the Web so assiduously that to this day sponsored ads for underwear of all descriptions crop up when I do online searches. Obviously, there is a marketer somewhere who thinks I am a personal-alert-device-wearing ninety-something-year-old who still likes sexy panties despite my bladder control problem. What a mess.

I couldn't find anything that might work in beige or nude, Mother's staples. I bought white ones, dipped them in a kitchen sink full of strong coffee to turn them ecru, and hung them to dry over the shower door in the hall bathroom.

Because they were designed to soak up lots of liquid, the drying process took forever. For days, whenever Herman ducked in for a quick trip, he was confronted by a thicket of dripping unmentionables. Even though he quit smoking in 1987, I fretted that in disgust he might go out to get a pack of cigarettes and never come back. I wouldn't have blamed him.

I worried about Mother's problem all the time and shared it with close friends and family.

"How's she doing?" they would ask.

"She has stopped wearing underwear," I would reply with details. I'm sure they thought I was the outlandish one.

The next time I went to see Mother nothing had changed, except that the staff had persuaded her to quit trying to rinse her own laundry. She had a plastic basket full of sopping undergarments in her bathroom and her room smelled awful . . . just the awful smell I had tried so hard to avoid when I was choosing a place for her to live.

I had made up my mind. I couldn't take her out again unless she wore panties and Poise. I told her so, as kindly but as firmly as I could.

She was furious.

She shook. She wagged her finger. She told me if that was the way I felt, she would just have dinner in and I could have dinner out and we could get together afterward.

I told her I enjoyed going to Red Lobster with her and that I hoped she would go but that she would have to wear appropriate underpinnings.

She pushed herself up out of her chair and stormed over to me, moving as quickly as a woman of her age can rampage.

I sat more firmly in my seat and waited for the outburst. I kept telling myself I could hold the line. I should hold the line.

"I'm an old lady," she said. "I don't have a problem and I can do whatever I want to do."

I repeated my stipulations like a mantra: First underwear. Then Red Lobster.

She gave in. Grudgingly.

"Oh, all right. I'll do it," she growled, "On one condition."

"What is that?"

"That it will make you deliriously happy."

Well, it didn't make me deliriously happy but

we did have our usual good time at the restaurant.

On the way home, halfway down the hall to her room, Mother stopped suddenly and turned to me.

"Oops," she said. "I don't think I quite made it."

Then she smiled, not slyly, but as though the whole drama had never happened. And she said the words that will forever be the end of this story: "I'm glad I had on underpants."

Chapter 3
Whatever You Do, Don't Remove the Tags

Here is how I plan to make it through old age: online shopping and prepaid return labels.

I will die a happy woman if I never have to go to a mall again.

A couple of years ago, I had to quit trying to take Mother there. It is too hazardous. For her health and mine.

She has one of those shiny rollators with the built-in seat. Handbrakes. Big wheels all around. No carved out tennis balls required to keep it moving smoothly.

Has one, but does not use it.

It is parked, abandoned, in the corner of her room in assisted living. The housekeeper dusts it regularly and recently someone piled a stack of paperwork in the basket to clear space for another framed family photo on Mother's desk. We tried, the nursing staff and I, to get her to rely on that fancy walker, but she is completely uncoachable when it comes to safety.

On hard, slippery floors in an open space— like a mall department store—she is terrifying. At this point, she has broken both hips and chipped a bone in her neck. She should not, under any circumstances, venture anywhere that is not lined with handrails and completely covered in soft foam rubber.

You try telling her.

She does deign to carry a cane and I do mean carry, like an accessory. It does about as much for her balance as a purse does for a tightrope walker.

Once, years ago, Mother told me that she thought elderly ladies with canes looked elegant. There is nothing particularly classy about the medical-grade aluminum hook with broad rubber stability tip that the physical therapist managed to get into Mother's hand. That doesn't faze her. Some of Mother's most unrealistic notions come from Depression-era movies featuring ditzy ingénues and wealthy older dames with ample bosoms, loops of pearls, and faux English accents.

I am pretty sure that is how she pictures herself, since every time she sets out she proclaims without fail, "I carry a cane but I don't need it."

To be honest, she probably would do just as well without it. She doesn't lean on it. She just waves it toward the ground like a drunk conducting an itty-bitty symphony orchestra. It is a flailing motion completely out of rhythm with her tottering, dodgy steps. A train wreck. NASCAR on a rainy track. Another fall waiting to happen.

Watching her walk is so alarming that onlookers can only hold their breath and dream up bad metaphors.

That's all I can do, anyway.

I mince alongside, holding her free hand gingerly, afraid to grip her arm for fear of upsetting whatever internal gyroscope propels her forward and keeps her upright. One day in the middle of Nordstrom—a retail temple where the floors are so icy slick I think they must do them with a Zamboni— I had an awful premonition. I saw myself holding aghast onto one of Mother's elbows while she dangled in a heap of osteoporotic bones at my feet.

That did it. No more excursions to broad slippery spaces with Mother.

My mother-in-law, on the other hand, terrorized me with brute energy.

For a few years early in our relationship, I was able to stave off shopping with Grannie. I don't even shop with girlfriends. I would much rather drink coffee, linger over lunch, chat, and people-watch together.

If I absolutely, positively cannot find what I need by catalog or website, I will make a once or twice a year dash through a couple of stores. Get in. Get out. Grab a bunch of stuff in what still might be my size if only I can manage to lay off the cookies. I cart it all home, try it on in the privacy of my bedroom, and make another sprint for returns.

Dawdling along *just looking* makes my lower back scream almost as loudly as the frustration I stifle so that no one calls Security.

In any case, when we were living in Kentucky, Grannie was visiting and wanted to go to Dillard's. She was 82. I was 45, although to be fair, I was learning to cope with a chronic illness, attending graduate school full time, and working at an assistantship. I existed day in and day out on the ragged edge of exhausted.

Even though she was older by nearly four decades, the sheer force of Grannie's personality, the drive of her will to conquer, and the methodical way she considered every single, solitary piece of clothing in the women's section left me so depleted that she had to find a chair so I could rest. She stood over me while I sat, rubbed my aching calves, and tried to catch my breath.

Maybe she was gloating. Maybe I was just feeling weak and defeated. I do know she has never let me forget it.

"She," Grannie says. She often calls me *she* in front of me. Heaven knows what she calls me behind my back. From time to time, in direct address, she calls me by my husband's first wife's nickname. "She," she says, "Has refused to go shopping with me ever since."

Darn tootin', I want to tell her.

I may be weak but I aspire to be a quick learner.

It is a skill I constantly try to hone in my Darwinian struggle with The Mothers.

Now that I am even older, I simply cannot push a wheelchair for either one of them. Grannie is beyond using a rollator for more than a hot minute and Macy's doesn't offer motorized carts like the big box stores. Herman could manage pushing the wheelchair but he has his limits. Up close to the top of his list is that he will not go anywhere near racks of dresses or ladies lingerie. Especially with his mother.

So if I am going to get into the act, both women unfortunately are stuck with whatever I can find for them.

Pray for us all.

Last spring, Grannie needed to do a stint in a physical rehab facility to get her strength back after a hospital stay. She said she didn't have a thing to wear. This is probably true, although she never gives anything away no matter how small or out of date it is. Her closet is jammed with things that will not work unless she loses thirty pounds or thirty years. Neither is going to happen.

I started at the discount places. Walmart. Kohl's. Target. There was nothing, not a single thing in her size that seemed suitable. She needed pants and tops for physical therapy and plenty of them.

I will admit that I blew it. To give her credit, Grannie always looks great when she dresses up: neat, well put together, and not a day over 85. She wears nice ensembles with jackets and pretty jewelry, and stuffs her poor aching feet into low-heeled pumps or sandals.

Regrettably, I was thinking *casual* with all the rules that a woman my age learned about what a woman her age should wear. Long sleeves. Long pants. Cover the ripples. Cover the dimples. Cover. Cover. Cover.

Not Grannie's rules. Around the house on a ninety-degree day with the windows open and no air conditioning, she is happy in capris and a short sleeve tee shirt. They must know this at the first three stores I tried, because that was all I found in her size.

On Day Two, I dragged myself to Belk—a large department store that is most popular in the South where we live and where I acquired those archaic wardrobe regulations. Belk had tons of things that I deemed perfectly proper and they were all on sale. Plus I had a coupon good for an all-day spree.

I took Grannie a nice pile of coordinates. She said she loved them and I believed it. *What big eyes you have, Grandma.*

Then for days—follow me now—she talked to me about how she had talked to someone else about the outrageous amount of money she thought I had spent.

"Aw, I can't imagine how anyone could spend that much on clothes," she said to my face, recounting her own part in my backstabbing. "Did you see those prices? They were so expensive."

I reminded her that everything was on sale and that she should ignore the printed price but she just kept going. I don't know which irked me more: losing two full days' worth of patience and energy doing something I hate or having her complain about it to someone else and then tell me that she had complained about it.

Despite her horror, Grannie snipped off the tags with a pair of scissors I had taken her and wore the clothes. It's a shame because if she hadn't, I could have put the whole haul back in the car and let her do her physical therapy in the underwear I also got for her. Which she liked.

I found it at Walmart.

Whatever you do, don't remove the tags. That's the first thing I learned when I had to start shopping with and for my own mother.

The second thing I learned is: Good luck with that.

The Anne Klein shoes felt fine in the store when the cute young salesman was batting his eyelashes at Mother. They pinch her toes unbearably just as soon as she has worn them once to the dentist and scuffed up the soles too much to return them. The twinset that the nurse's aide flattered her into wearing by telling her it makes her eyes look like emeralds will languish in the closet for eternity just as soon as Mother's name and room number are written in indelible laundry ink on the neck label.

I always fall for that brief joyful moment of expectation when Mother seems truly pleased with a new outfit, when I think she is finally going to ditch this year's raggedy skirt and food-stained top and wear something clean, unrumpled, and still attractive.

Then the bubble bursts.

As a result Mother has a stuffed closet of her own, full of truly expensive, barely worn yet ruined pieces of clothing that cannot be returned, donated, or liquidated. She will not shop anywhere but Nordstrom and fancy label or not, clothing will not be accepted for consignment if it is marked with her moniker like a kid's camp shirts. Even Goodwill ships her things off for rags since the one time she wore them she invariably launched a tasting menu of her dinner down the front.

Back when he was in office and had to disclose his tax returns, Bill Clinton made himself the butt of a month's worth of Jay Leno monologues by deducting some $2 pairs of underpants as a charitable contribution.

I feel his pain.

At least Goodwill took the presidential Fruit of the Loom. I assume they did not have "Leader of the Free World" inked on every waistband.

To tell you the truth, it is heartbreaking. Before her mind completely sabotaged her, Mother always looked like a Talbots model. She bought a few things of good quality and put them together beautifully. A challis skirt or raw silk pants. An ivory

31

charmeuse blouse. A boiled wool jacket or cashmere sweater. Black patent pumps. Pearls. A perfect haircut.

To this day, I cannot wear a ruffled silk blouse without my husband giving me an appraising hairy eyeball and saying, "I don't really like that. You look too much like your mother." Soon, I suppose I will get the same reaction from a pilled sweater with a week's worth of meals ground into the knitwork.

A couple of years ago, accompanied by an aide from assisted living, Mother went to the eye doctor that she has been seeing for the last decade. He called me in horror when she left, certain that I had no idea of the condition of her clothes and the fact that she was wearing talcum powder-covered bedroom slippers with a hole in one big toe. Or maybe he was certain that I did know and was simply neglecting her.

How could I tell him how hard I had tried to find something else—anything else—she would wear? How many horribly expensive pieces of silk and cashmere and merino wool the personal shopper had brought into the dressing room? How few Mother had agreed to take home and how many fewer she ever wore more than once? How many websites I had pored over? How many outfits I had taken to her, cajoled her to try on, and found hanging in the closet—yes, the tags still on them— the next time I visited, and the next, and the next?

So here are my new rules: Clip the tags. Toss the receipts. Just be sure to get all the clothes at a supercenter. Why spend a bundle when *a)* It is just going to get me bad-mouthed or *b)* The clothes will never be worn anyway?

Besides, I can always stop in the candy and cookie aisles to stock up for the binge I will have when all that shopping goes for naught. Have you tried the new pretzel M&M's? They are downright addicting.

Chapter 4
Where I Live They Have Bibs

I have given up on The Mothers and the mall but my husband and I still take them out for dinner when we are in the mood to be embarrassed. Dining out with either one is a recipe for mortification. As the father of three now-grown children, Herman at least has had practice with loud, rambunctious tablemates. Me, not so much. We tip heavily to keep the servers from spitting in our soup next time. There is nothing we can do to keep the noise down for the guests seated around us.

It is a vicious cycle. We try to choose places where couples won't be expecting a quiet romantic evening, but the decibel level in family friendly restaurants is already high. Add background racket to the tinnitus The Mothers hear in their own deafened ears and dinner is a heck of a commotion.

Deciding what to eat is a shouting match. "What are you having?" Mother yells, and then cannot hear a word I say unless I scream it back. The last time we went out, I asked the server for a stack of blank order slips and simply took to writing my answers for Mother.

Not that it matters. When the meal comes, we have both forgotten what we asked for. I have to holler it all over again. The last time we went to Red Lobster, we shared a salad with blue cheese dressing on the side for her and vinaigrette for me. Somewhere along the way, Mother totally lost the concept and started eating her dressing out of the container with a spoon.

"This is delicious," she said. "What is it again?"

What could I say?

"Glad you like it," I roared.

Of course, it dribbles on the table, in her lap, and all over her clothes, leaving crusty white streaks and blobs on her customarily black sweater.

Sometimes I suggest that we tuck our napkins in under our chins. This, she drummed into me as a child, is absolutely tacky in public and frowned upon at home if you are over the age of five.

That was then. This is now. For a while before she moved into assisted living, Mother was in a skilled nursing home where the meals were served in a dining room to those who were well enough to congregate there. Some residents needed help with feeding. Almost all were shaky. Before they began, everyone got a large terry cloth cover tied around their necks.

While she was staying at the nursing home, the first time we went out to dinner, I unwrapped my silverware and placed my napkin in my lap. Mother remarked in a booming voice, "Where I live, we have bibs." Everyone turned toward the source of the outburst. Thank goodness, no one pointed.

I also have to admire the restraint of the other diners at Red Lobster who didn't yell along with me that the third nonalcoholic cocktail Mother had just drained to the slurping bottom with her straw was *fruit punch*. I couldn't bring myself to try to explain *Virgin* or *Mai Tai* at the top of my lungs in a crowd.

My mother-in-law, Grannie, is also an

announcer. She is prone to share with everyone around us whatever misadventure she has had in the ladies room. At least she was only at McDonald's when she returned from the restroom and belted out, "I sat down and couldn't get up." Herman probably would have crawled under the table if he didn't have a phobia about dirty floors.

There must be something about McDonald's that breaks down inhibitions. And the acoustics are better than the Mormon Tabernacle.

My mother had her own Mickey D's moment. She was riding along with Herman and me to my cousin's home in South Carolina for Christmas. I was in the backseat. Mother was in the front with Herman.

He doesn't have much patience for the repetitious conversation that is an inevitable outcome of short-term memory loss. So after about the twentieth time Mother remarked that the oncoming traffic was heavy and at least the tenth that she asked him if he enjoyed driving, Herman decided he needed a break.

He found a shopping center, dropped Mother and me off to get a couple of Happy Meals, and went to drive through a car wash for a brief respite.

Needless to say, Mother and I created our usual sideshow.

In the first place, our relationship is as clear as the noses on our faces and the shape of our smiles. We cannot walk three feet without somebody remarking how much alike we look, even though I am five-foot-nine and she has settled at about five feet flat. What with our clearly being ancient mother and practically as ancient child and my shouting about the cheeseburgers and her hollering about the fries, we were the center of attention for the African-American man and his family who were seated nearby.

To fully appreciate just what happened next, you need to know that my husband is also African American. I am not. I wish I could tell you that our interracial relationship was never an issue for Mother, but that would be a lie. Today, she thinks Herman is the cat's pajamas and rarely fails to tell me how glad she is that I have found a good husband and have a happy marriage. It took her a few years.

In any case, Mother is not, as they say,

colorblind. Herman's race is always lodged at some deep level in her perception of him.

We had just finished eating and were throwing away our trash when I saw him driving up outside.

"We need to go now," I said. "Herman is coming."

Blank look. *What?*

"It's time to go. Herman is coming."

The light dawned, a mental connection was made, a synapse fired, and Mother raucously began to sing a classic but horrifically culturally insensitive Stephen Foster number.

"I'm coming. I'm coming," she caterwauled. "For my head is bending low."

My head was bending low and my face was turning bright red.

Out of the corner of my eye, I caught the glance of the man at the neighboring table. I grimaced. He smiled back at me with a look of understanding, which I will appreciate until the day I die. Because we both knew what else was coming and it was coming at the top of her lungs.

"I hear the gentle voices calling," Mother

finished with a flourish as she toddled toward the door, "Old. Black. Joe."

Chapter 5

There Must Be Something
Wrong with This Phone

Apparently the Direct Marketing Association has a database that lists Herman and me as consumers of helpful tools to improve the lives of the elderly and decrepit. Occasionally we receive catalogs of adaptive equipment and other stuff that looks intriguing. I always identify a dozen promising items for The Mothers and sometimes see something interesting for myself as well.

Okay, so at 59, I'm in moderately good shape. It just feels as though I am 100. In any case, I am making a pact with myself right now that when the time comes, I will embrace a small, smart hearing aid; a big button telephone with an amplifier; a lift chair; and any other device that computer chips and the mind of entrepreneurs can contribute to keeping me engaged and mobile. I have seen what happens when The Mothers slough off all the things that Herman and I hunt down and present to them with such hope in our hearts.

This winter, I broke my foot on a trip to Florida. I didn't hesitate to grab a motorized scooter everywhere one was offered. Apparently I was quite a sight. Tooling through the produce department of a Key West supermarket in a straw hat, peach cargo shorts, and big black orthopedic boot, I caught a man watching me. I shrugged, smiled, and remarked, "Heck of a way to spend a vacation."

"Yes, girl," he replied. "But you make it look cute."

That'll work.

Maybe that is what we have needed all along to get The Mothers to graciously accept all the gear we have bought for them . . . a good-looking, kind of fey, middle-aged guy to egg them on.

If only they could hear him.

Thanks to Herman's father's thirty hard years as a coal miner and his union survivor benefits, Grannie has been blessed with extraordinary insurance that supplements her Medicare and pays for necessities like shower chairs, rollators, glasses, and the inevitable hearing aid. And thanks to Herman's persistence and patience dealing with bureaucracies, vendors, and doctors' offices, she has them.

Does she use them?

You tell me.

Grannie lived with us for awhile, which meant in the evenings when we came home from work, she was more or less a permanent fixture in one of the two armchairs in our open-plan kitchen. One night I was working on supper when I began to hear a chirping that didn't stop and that sounded like the kind of signal that needed attention. It seemed to be coming from the direction of Grannie's chair, but there was no device over there to emit that kind of warning.

"Grannie," I said loudly and distinctly, "Do you hear a beeping?"

"Hunh?"

"Do you HEAR a BEEPING?"

Nope. Nope. Nothing.

It was so persistent and so strongly from her direction that I figured my own hearing was finally going, that one ear had blown out, and I had lost my ability to tell exactly where sound was coming from.

I turned off the burner under dinner and checked the smoke and carbon monoxide detectors on the first floor. They were fine, and even though I knew it was nuts, I looked at the ones in the basement, too. I pushed all the buttons on the microwave. I tried my laptop and Herman's computer. I turned off the TV and turned it on again. I opened the garage door and listened to the parked, silent cars. I even considered calling our security alarm monitoring center to see if there was something hidden somewhere that could be so relentless.

Half-browned chicken cooled in the pan on the stove, getting greasier by the minute.

"Grannie, are you sure you don't hear anything?"

The noise seemed to be coming from her lap . . . from the closed fist in her lap. I entered the Twilight Zone and said, "What do you have in your hand?"

"Oh that," she said. "That's my hearing aid. I took it out."

And there it sat, in the palm of her hand, nagging frantically to alert her that it had been removed and not turned off. I could have polished off a bag of Lorna Doone cookies all by myself right then but they would have spoiled my dinner.

At least Grannie does have a hearing aid, even though she leaves it in the box, plops it down on a table and forgets it, or drops it while trying to put it in and sits on it far more often than she wears it.

Mother simply refused.

She has had her hearing checked twice in the last few years.

The first time, we could still have a relatively coherent conversation on the phone.

The audiologist, Mother reported, had recommended a discreet, state-of-the-art device, which included the latest electronics to help sort out the sounds she was missing, rather than just making everything indiscriminately louder.

"I am not going to get it," she said, in a *that's final* tone that I know intimately. "It is three thousand dollars." This from a woman who five years before would buy an authentic antique Persian rug or have a chair recovered in expensive linen with down-filled cushions simply because she was bored.

"Really, Mother," I wanted to say, "This is no time to become fiscally conservative."

"What?" she would have said, "What risky alternative?"

Never mind.

By the time Mother made her next visit to have her hearing tested, it had deteriorated terribly. I got the results from the specialist directly, since phone interactions had become a jumble of misunderstood words, repeating myself, and Mother abruptly switching gears in the middle of a discussion. I had learned that the introductory phrase *on another subject* means that she has not understood a word I have just said and so she is barging forward with a new conversational gambit . . . usually something we have already talked about just two minutes before.

Herman listens to my end of things and shakes his head. "You and your mother," he says, as though I can do anything about it except hang up and pretend we have gotten disconnected. Try explaining that when she rings back.

In any case, the last time she went, Mother called from the audiologist's office to have me get the latest report from the horse's mouth. The professional's opinion was that it was probably too late for a hearing aid. He had tested for ability to hear raw sound and tested for comprehension. Mother was struggling with both. She no longer has the manual dexterity to handle such a tiny piece of equipment and has such a resistance to anything new that it would have just been money down the drain. But an amplifying telephone especially designed for the hard of hearing might make talking long distance easier, the technician said. They used one right there in the office.

Aha. No wonder Mother had been able to understand me so easily a few moments before.

I hung up and went straight to Amazon.com. I examined the illustrations to find a phone that looked most like the one Mother already had, with jumbo buttons and a corded handset. I combed the specifications for the phone that was easiest to use, that could be set to amplify all the time without any input from Mother. I read hundreds of reviews, paying particular attention to those written by adult children who, like me, were buying for recalcitrant parents.

I found a suitable model for about $150, sent it to the attention of the director of the assisted living facility, and asked her to have the new phone installed in place of Mother's old one.

Five days later, my phone rang.

It was Mother and she was hopping mad.

"Someone has come and given me a new telephone," she ranted, "AND I DO. NOT. WANT. IT."

"I arranged that, Mother," I said. "I hoped you would like being able to hear more clearly and we could have better conversations."

Miracle of miracles, she understood me perfectly.

"I don't need it," she said. "I don't want it. I like the old one. Maybe I have a little trouble understanding people sometimes, but they'll just have to repeat themselves."

I don't know if she heard me sigh deeply or if she thought it was a windy defect of the new phone. I don't know who she bullied into removing it and reinstalling the old one. I am sure she didn't do it herself.

Of course no one thought to save the packaging or to ask me whether I wanted to try to return the whole expensive apparatus. By the time the entire drama played out, it was too late anyway. Another $150 wasted and all I got was another anecdote.

I do have to tip my hat to whoever decided where to stow the new phone after it was disconnected. The next time I was there, I found it in the top dresser drawer, nestled among Mother's rejected pink and black Walmart underwear, knee-high stockings in their original packages, and a host of other things I have bought that she has set aside with disdain.

Perfect. Mother may not have wanted to use her newfangled telephone, but I certainly got the message.

Chapter 6

All Those Old Ladies Are in Wheelchairs

My husband, Herman, and I quickly learned that anyone who does research on how to ease an elder's transition to safer, more manageable housing had better bring along a salt shaker. It takes more than a single grain to season everything the experts dish up and expect adult children to swallow.

For example:

Sit down with your parents before there is a crisis.

Observe their home and routines.

Listen.

Have a calm loving talk about the challenges of maintaining their current residence and lifestyle.

Offer options.

Be firm but understanding.

And our contribution: *Expect to get your*

head handed to you, bloodied and reeling.

I am sorry to say that if anything pushes us to divorce after all these years, it will be my mother-in-law, Grannie, and her staunch refusal to look at her situation, face reality, and get more help than Herman can provide on a day-to-day basis.

Please don't misunderstand. I am crazy about Herman. I love him so much that I cannot bear the idea of living without him. Since Grannie is driving him to his death of aggravation, it has gotten to the point where the only choices left to me are to bite my tongue raw when she acts up or to nag him not to let her kill him with hardheadedness.

That thing you smell burning in our household is tension.

The horrific tussle over living arrangements with my own mother eventually left me lying in the hospital myself recovering from a stress-induced heart episode.

Sometimes I wonder just who is living in la-la land.

Us?

The Mothers?

Or the bloggers, authors, and magazine

editors who ladle up the hogwash that elderly parents will cheerfully agree to move to a senior apartment or come to stay with a worried middle-aged child without a miserable fight?

When I am not feeling like I have just gone five rounds in a small cage with a wild animal, I do understand that The Mothers have already faced more change than they can manage. They are the last living sibling of each of their birth families. Every day—every minute—another faculty goes awry or some body part that was working yesterday suddenly begins to leak, ache, or falter. They no longer have the mental capacity to find their way in unfamiliar places or to adapt to new situations . . . in Mother's case especially.

You can teach an old lady new tricks if you have the patience but you will certainly get barked at and probably bitten.

Herman has a canine expression that used to capture Grannie's attitude perfectly. "Oh, she'll go," he said, when he packed her up and moved her to our hometown from the deserted mountain coal camp where she had lived for more than ninety years. "But she's going with her claws in the sidewalk."

Now that Grannie needs the additional support of assisted living, she has dug in completely and decided that she will stay in the apartment right where she is, even if she cannot walk, cook, get herself safely to the bathroom, or raise her arms to dress without yelping in pain.

If he had not died of drink at age 39, which tells me all I need to know, I could cheerfully shoot Dylan Thomas, the Welsh poet who wrote "Do Not Go Gentle into That Good Night." You know the poem, inspired by Thomas's father who was infirm and going blind. *Old age should burn and rave at close of day; Rage, rage, against the dying of the light.*

Maybe.

I would bet Thomas never spent a single moment with brochures spread out on the kitchen table, pleading with his father to move somewhere that he would not fall down the stairs. Again.

When I hear those blasted verses, all I can think about is one of The Mothers with her metaphorical fingers in her ears, shutting her eyes, and chanting *blah, blah, blah* like a five-year-old refusing broccoli.

Go ahead. Burn and rave. But not at *us*. Honestly, Mother, we only want to help without driving ourselves into an early grave in the process.

I feel for Herman's kids—my three stepchildren—if this resistance turns out to be genetic. One son has already moved to Dubai. He loves us. I know he does. But I am not completely sure about his motivation to head halfway around the world and leave his brother and sister holding the short stick.

There are certainly indicators that if I survive long enough, I will be difficult to dislodge.

My grandmother—Mother's mother—was small, soft, a wonderful cook with a sweet tooth as voracious as my own, and childlike herself. She was prone to burp loudly at the dinner table and then laugh uproariously.

I adored her.

When I was growing up, she lived a couple of blocks away from her small town's Baptist Home for seniors. She herself was a devoted churchgoing Baptist and the longtime widow of a Baptist minister. He was twenty-five years older than

Grandmother, a story for another day. He died when she was in her early fifties and left her behind to live alone for years on a miniscule pension in their modest, paid-for house. Somehow she managed with great aplomb.

Grandmother in fact went to work at the Baptist Home for a few years when she was sixty-something and probably as old as or older than a good third of the residents. She didn't move in herself until she was 92. Clearly, she had no objection to the place on religious grounds, but from the time I was small, I remember the family chuckling indulgently about her description of its residents. She called them *those old ladies*.

This was ironically funny even to me, with my six-year-old sense of humor, since Grandmother was the oldest person I knew.

Who's laughing now?

My own mother's journey through the landscape of elder housing has been—typically for her—backwards and downright bizarre. At every stop, she has bucked and complained that she didn't belong where she was while also refusing to move to something more appropriate.

"I never should have let you bring me here," she used to gripe every single time we talked or I visited.

Now she only says it when she is having a bad day.

It began in 2002 when I started campaigning for her to move from her townhouse into a nearby continuing care community.

Continuing care communities offer a progression of living arrangements, depending on a resident's age and capacity for self-care. The levels range from totally independent villas and apartments, to the semi-independent studio apartments where Mother eventually made her initial landing, on to assisted living, and finally to a skilled nursing pavilion for the acutely or extremely ill and a memory care center for residents in advanced stages of Alzheimer's or dementia.

At first, I could not convince Mother to leave her own two-story home in an isolated community in the middle of nowhere, even though her doctor said she needed supervision 24/7. At the time, she was burning through tens of thousands of dollars in long term care insurance and cash in order for me to pay someone to come in and cook, clean, help her with personal care, check on her medication, and watch her day and night.

I pleaded with her. Think about the future. She would need funds for a down payment to get a nice place in a more suitable setting. She had already broken one hip. What if she fell again? How would she make it to her upstairs bedroom?

Every time I brought it up, she went all Scarlet O'Hara on me. *Fiddle-dee-dee.* She pursed her lips, tossed her head and said, "I'll worry about that when it happens."

One day it did happen. There was a terrible ice storm at Mother's. The nighttime aide bailed. The daytime helper could not make it in over the frozen roads. I called Mother from my work nearly 300 miles away every hour on the hour to make sure she was okay.

As lunchtime neared, she became distressed. No one had made her usual yogurt and sandwich. What should she do?

I had her take the phone to the pantry and tell me what was there.

Soup, she said. "But how would I get it

warm?"

Despite the weather, the electricity was still on, as was the gas. I didn't dare tell her to use the stove.

That was the day I began working with her doctor to invoke Mother's power of attorney and take care of her more assertively. The geriatric care manager who had been helping me coordinate Mother's aides long-distance planned the move with me.

The continuing care community I had scouted out—call it Happy Acres—assessed Mother and determined she would do well in their assisted living. It is in a spacious, nicely decorated building with large rooms and bright sunlight, a lovely dining room with hardwood floors, tall windows and tables for four, a community parakeet, piano, widescreen TV, and beautiful gardens.

The area is behind locked double doors, though, to protect residents who lose their way outside of familiar surroundings. I could not imagine that Mother would ever in a million years accept that particular state of affairs.

As usual I was wrong.

Rational.

But wrong.

I settled instead on a less restrictive, semi-independent studio with a small kitchen, shared dining room with prepared meals. It offered more freedom, plus a staff member on call day and night.

For the first few weeks after Mother's relocation, I planned to continue hiring one of the aides who had been working at the townhouse, just to ease them both through the adjustment.

On D-Day, the geriatric care manager took Mother to a long lunch while Herman and a moving crew helped me arrange a selection of Mother's things in the apartment. While I was shoving around a sofa, the aide I had been counting on to get Mother over the rough patches announced that she had decided to become a hairdresser. She quit on the spot, asked for a check, and left.

I didn't have the energy to stalk her to the parking lot, hijack the moving van, and run over her.

Herman went home. I called my boss and stayed at Happy Acres myself for almost a week, introducing Mother to the other residents, and coaching her on the surroundings, schedules, and culture. My role model was a wise old college sophomore camp counselor who had nursed me through wrenching homesickness the summer I was eleven.

The strategy seemed to work.

Then, a few nights after I left, at one thirty on the morning of my fiftieth birthday, the phone rang. I took it in the bathroom so I could talk without disturbing Herman.

Mother was in the hospital. The care manager who had helped me arrange the transition was with her. She reported that Mother had been found on the floor in her room disoriented and dehydrated. She would not eat, drink, or take her medication.

It has been almost ten years since that call, but I still remember that when I hung up, I sat on the side of the tub and sobbed. For both of us. For all of us. For my vulnerable yet impossible Mother, because I was just beginning to comprehend the depth of her dysfunction. For my patient but neglected husband. And for me.

I realized I was merely at the start of an arduous, rocky journey; I thought I had just finished it.

Mother was released from the hospital to recover for a few days in the only skilled nursing bed Happy Acres had immediately available. It was in the securely locked Alzheimer's section, where every resident wore an alarm bracelet in case she strayed. They put one on Mother's wrist and assured me they would keep her there only until she got rehydrated and reoriented.

She stayed five years of her own free will.

Happy Acres still tried to convince her to go into assisted living. They took her on outings with other residents. They invited her to lunch in the dining room. They showed her a series of sunny rooms that overlooked the gardens.

Mother simply refused to consider it. She wanted to go home. Otherwise, she said she was fine right where she was. She complained that *those old ladies* in the Alzheimer's unit were not very sociable: She never did seem to grasp their condition. Still, she liked some of their grown children, the members of the staff, and the view of a courtyard from her wall of windows.

I supported her, Heaven help me. I could not bear for her to endure another unsuccessful move and potential breakdown.

Finally, Mother got so incensed with impaired residents wandering into her room and napping on her bed that she began to shove and slap at them. Happy Acres moved her to another skilled nursing area.

She wanted to go back to the Alzheimer's unit even though she seemed to thrive in the next setting.

"I never should have had to move here," she said, although for meals she sat at a table with people who could carry on a conversation and were cognizant enough to raise their voices so she could hear. She had a blushing crush on a handsome young man on the staff, confiding he might be married, she wasn't sure. He and some woman he talked about had just had a third child. That and the ring on his left hand were the giveaway, I guess.

Among the residents, she made a few friends. Not that she belonged with them. "All those old ladies are in wheelchairs. I am *not* in a wheelchair," she would say with conviction.

Then her insurance and savings ran completely out. All that was left was my father's monthly survivor benefit. The amount was generous enough to fund Mother's three earlier trips to Europe but fell far short of the cost of the skilled nursing unit where she was now ensconced.

Happy Acres stood firm. On her budget, Mother's choices were a less expensive room in assisted living or a grocery cart and the street.

It took her a year to completely master the routine and layout of assisted living but since Mother she finally arrived there she has been relatively content.

"How are you doing?" I shout, when I visit.

"Oh," she'll laugh, and she looks so much like her own sweet little mother that it's scary. Scary like in a movie where you know that precious child on the screen in reality is possessed by the devil.

"Oh," she'll laugh, and then she says the same thing every time. "I'm doing pretty well for an old lady."

Chapter 7
Doctor, I Know Best

The time came when we decided that Herman needed professional assistance girding his loins.

We had been so distressed and bogged down in his—so far unsuccessful—struggle to get his mother, Grannie, moved to safer ground that we had been snapping at each other. A lot. We thought a disinterested yet knowledgeable person could encourage him, keep us from wrangling between ourselves when we should be wrangling with Grannie, and suggest some strategies that have worked for other sons in his shoes.

Third parties never come cheap. We paid the only geriatric care manager in our town $90 per hour for a two and a half hour consultation at our kitchen table. Just the two of us and the care manager for now.

The first half hour was free. This was good since we spent it bellyaching. Herman groused about Grannie. I threw in a couple of tales about my mother and her own move to assisted living so the care manager would understand we are not newbies. We have already tried everything.

Once we got past the war stories, the care manager shared information she had brought with her. She left it behind in a very slick-looking packet. That afternoon, thumbing through, I saw that she had shown us all the materials except for a colorfully illustrated, bound book in large print, *Talking to Your Doctor: A Guide for Older People.*

I guess she had quickly realized it would be a waste to bring it up. From our sighs, rolled eyes, and diatribes, she could tell The Mothers wouldn't pay the slightest bit of attention.

Kind of like they treat the doctor.

Oh, Grannie knows how to talk *about* her doctor. In the time I have known her she has not been to a single one who wasn't just trying to find something wrong with her so he could rake in more money for himself and his cronies.

This theory has never kept her from going.

Before she came to live near us, one of the high points of her social life involved navigating her 1992 Cadillac two hours roundtrip on hazardous Appalachian mountain roads for appointments with the nearest family physician, "Doc," and whatever specialist he recommended next.

I don't know whether Doc indeed had a hankering for a Cadillac of his own or whether Grannie's eighty-plus-year run of ironclad health just ran out. All of a sudden, it seemed like she did need a lot of medical intervention.

Within the span of a couple of years, she got a bad case of the flu, cataracts that ripened to the point of removal, a kidney infection that rendered her delirious, nightly acid reflux that caused her to erupt like Vesuvius soon after she lay down, and more.

I know a lot of this because for the first five years that she lived nearby, until I washed my hands of it and she was relieved to see me quit, I had been the one to accompany Grannie on medical appointments.

It is Herman's belief that any time a woman who is not your own wife has to go to the doctor and would like a companion, the best person for the job is another woman. He calls us *ladies*. I think he is terrified that if he gets in the examining room and cannot get out, he will see or hear something that scars him permanently.

One afternoon I came home to find he wasn't there. In his place was a whiff of rushed departure.

You get good at sniffing out urgency when you have as much experience with elder crises as we have.

I was afraid that something had happened to Grannie and when I reached Herman on his mobile phone, sure enough, there was a medical emergency. But it was our neighbor. She had had a bad reaction to her allergy shots and Herman had raced her back to the allergist for treatment.

"I don't feel right about this," he said over the phone. He sounded panicky. "Can you come sit with her?"

Of course. When I got there, Herman was in his car in the parking lot and our neighbor was apparently in the doctor's office.

"Is she okay? What are you doing out here?" I asked.

"I think she's fine," he said. "But you really should go in there. I'm going home. She needs another lady." He threw the car into reverse and bolted.

I don't know what it is that is so gender-specific about anaphylactic shock, but apparently he does. Perhaps he should write a book called *Ladies and Their Delicate Conditions*.

In any case, as another lady, I can tell you from eyewitness experience that a doctor's exam of Grannie is an exercise in futility. They ought to charge her with Medicare fraud.

Even if she is so sick or sore that she can barely get into the car and to the office, suddenly when the physician walks in, everything is hunky dory. He couldn't get a straight answer out of her with thumb screws.

It frustrates the doctor.

It frustrates me.

It drives Herman occasionally to drink huge slugs of Johnnie Walker on very few rocks.

"You won't believe what she did," he said one afternoon, when he finally returned from an arduous day accompanying Grannie and the rescue squad to the emergency room for what turned out *not* to be a stroke, thank goodness.

"When the paramedics got her down to the lobby, she waved," Herman said, staring balefully into his glass. "She sat up on the gurney and waved at everyone on the way out of the apartment building. 'Bye. I'm going on my vacation,' she said."

I was with her in 2005 when the doctor first told Grannie to put her feet up to keep the blood from pooling around her ankles and causing them to swell, get infected, and turn reddish-purple.

That was seven years ago. Last month, Herman came home from checking on her one afternoon and reported, "She finally had her feet up."

He had a drink to celebrate.

Unlike Grannie, Mother is usually quite cooperative during doctor visits. It is only after she leaves that the trouble begins.

She either forgets or ignores whatever they tell her—unless they give her such outrageously inappropriate advice that it is tantamount to malpractice. Then she is all over it.

A couple of years ago, she rolled out of bed in

her sleep. Another daughter probably would have sued the facility. Honestly, if I cannot get her to wear underpants, how are they going to manage to put up her side rails? She is in assisted living, not a penitentiary. Residents have a federally-mandated right to be as independent as they possibly can and to refuse treatment. Mother landed flat on her face when she fell and chipped the wing on a vertebra in her neck.

After a sweet and extraordinarily gentle trauma care nurse talked her into putting on an orthopedic collar, Mother was released from the ER. The collar drove Mother crazy and with good reason. It looked like a piece of body jewelry in an anthropology museum, some sort of tribal neck stretcher, only in white plastic with straps that fastened with Velcro. It was designed to rest on her shoulders and under her chin, holding the upper spine immobile. She could not eat more than a spoonful of food per meal because she could not see over it down to her plate. And it looked like it chafed.

"They tell me I have to wear this," she said with disgust. "But nobody knows how to put it on right."

That might have been correct. Someone had written *front* on it in black indelible ink, which alone would have driven me up the wall. It was hideous enough as it was. Once she was strapped in, Mother wriggled around like Houdini until it loosened, defeating the purpose. Finally she figured out the Velcro and that was all she wrote. The dreadful contraption came off and stayed off.

I wanted to suggest cotton padding, a pretty scarf to cover the ugliness, anything, but I knew that nothing would work. I could not get her to understand that she had a broken bone and that the treatment was to keep the bone in place until it could mend. Any adult would have understood that explanation. Even many people with dementia would have understood if it was accompanied by a drawing with all the parts labeled. Not Mother.

I consulted the geriatric orthopedist who had first seen Mother at the nearby prestigious university hospital. He recommended surgery but I could not wrangle enough information out of him to make an informed decision.

My cousin—who has had neck problems of

her own—helped research the surgical options. We learned that the vertebra could be stabilized permanently but that the operation would require harvesting a piece of bone from Mother's hip.

Which hip? Both are artificial.

Recovery entailed six weeks' post-surgical treatment in, *tah-dah,* an orthopedic collar.

Hello? I wondered, my teeth clenched. *Was the doctor even listening?*

I crossed my fingers and decided to leave the healing in God's hands.

So far, so good. If you ask Mother how her neck is today, she will say, "Why, what happened?"

A few years ago, she was seen by a dermatologist at the same nationally famous facility. Mother had hives and, *oh by the way,* while she was there, she asked for a referral to a plastic surgeon to get a new breast implant. At the time, she was 84. The skin doctor obliged her.

Many years ago, Mother had a cancer scare. She had a single mastectomy and a simultaneous then-highly-experimental implant procedure. Amazingly, the whole thing held up fine for a quarter of a century. Then, one day Mother called me in an uproar.

They—whoever *they* were—had insisted, she said, that she do some kind of overhead maneuver in an exercise class at the nursing home and her implant had collapsed. I never did get a clear picture of what happened. I am pretty sure it did not involve bench pressing or Olympic style squats and thrusts, but to hear Mother tell it, it was equally strenuous.

I am also confident that it was time and not strain that caused the implant to finally flatten. I never convinced Mother of that either. Nor could I sell her on wearing the costly custom prosthetic form that I immediately set in motion.

In my mind, it was the only solution. I could not fathom that any medical professional would even discuss implantation surgery on a woman old enough to be his great-grandmother. The possibility of overhearing something like that is probably why Herman does his best to stay the heck out of it.

I don't know what was on the dermatologist's mind. Maybe he was hoping Mother would just forget the whole thing by the time she left the office. If that was his strategy, then he should not have written down the name and telephone number of the plastic surgeon on a prescription form and given it to Mother.

I saw the referral in the pile of papers that Mother keeps on her nightstand to remind her of things that she wants to remember but knows are beyond her at this point. She keeps envelopes from old Christmas and birthday cards and letters that she still intends to answer, although if they get separated from the correspondence itself, she cannot remember which is which. She keeps things that come in the mail to Occupant. And she kept the dermatologist's prescription slip.

When I asked her about it, unfortunately, that reminded her that she wanted to make an appointment with the surgeon to discuss an implant. The next week, she did, and called to tell me that she had done so. Thank goodness I had tucked his name away in some still-functioning corner of my own mind.

I tracked down his practice on the Web, called the office, explained the situation, and cancelled the consultation. Mother got in the habit of stuffing a wad of tissue in her bra. The prosthesis sat unworn and out of sight in a box. When she moved from the Alzheimer's unit to a more appropriate placement a few years later, she left it behind and never looked back.

I can only imagine how it must have thoroughly bewildered the poor woman—or Heaven forbid, man—with dementia who moved into Mother's old room. What must he have thought? And did the staff even believe him when he told them that he had found a modestly sized, perfectly formed breast at the back of his closet shelf.

Chapter 8

S-E-X and the Single Nonagenarian

One evening last year, my mother told me what she liked most about her new 90-year-old boyfriend.

"He's affectionate," she said, craning her neck to look up at me, "But not mushy."

She was the happiest I had seen her in years. I wasn't completely sure what she meant, though. He kisses her cheek but doesn't recite bad poetry?

I didn't pursue it. She cannot hear three-quarters of what I say. We were walking down the hall so I could not scribble my end of the conversation on a notepad for her to read.

And some part of me knew I would be better off to leave it alone.

Mother has always been an outrageous, yet oddly childlike, flirt. She has a saucy way of standing with one toe sort of pointed, swaying a pushed-out hip and looking up from under her upper eyelashes. Even at 91, she's quite a Lolita.

I am woefully familiar with that stance. It was the one she took when she tried on my college boyfriend's leather jacket forty years ago, cocked her head just so, and breathed up at him how big it was.

Two is company.

Three is a crowd.

Suddenly it got mighty crowded in our front hall and I was the extraneous one.

I didn't know whether to run upstairs and slam my bedroom door or to ask her to show me how to knock a young man all giddy like that.

I didn't do either. It has never been wise to challenge my mother and Heaven knows we have never confided in each other about S-E-X.

I would like to keep it that way.

The nursing staff at the assisted living facility had another idea.

One of them cornered me on my way out that night.

"Do you know what's going on with your mother and Mr. X?" she asked.

"He's affectionate but not mushy?" I ventured, warily.

"He is an exhibitionist and he has tried to put his hands on every woman in the place," she said. "The only one who hasn't rebuffed him is your mother. He's all over her in public. Right here in the living room. And she's letting him. It's making the other residents uncomfortable."

I knew how they felt.

I could hear the next sentence coming, too, and I wasn't about to get put on the spot.

What in the world, in all of their experience with my mother, would make that staff think I have any influence whatsoever?

I cannot get Mother to brush her teeth with her special toothpaste, change her sweater, or wear underpants. Do they really think I will be able to successfully suggest that she and Mr. X keep their knobby fingers to themselves?

Call me a dreadful daughter, but oddly, it does not bother me that Mother engages in whatever it is that she does with him.

That is her business. As long as she does not throw one of her hip replacements out of joint, I am glad she has someone to love her.

For Heaven's sake, what is the worst that will happen? She'll get pregnant?

No. The worst that will happen is that I will have to have the sex talk.

I made it through my teens without it and I do not want to start now.

Before the nurse could ask if I would approach Mother about her behavior, I made a pre-emptive strike.

"What are you doing about it?" I asked.

"We tell him he can do whatever she consents to in private, but they will have to go to his room or hers. It makes him really angry and he refuses to go. He just acts more defiant and she lets him."

"Gosh, maybe the administrator can help," I said, and ran for the exit.

Please don't make me tell my mother and her lover to get a room, I thought as I dodged toward the door.

I knew Mother had a crush on Mr. X.

Last January, a few months before the "mushy" talk, my cousins, our husbands, and I held a ninetieth birthday party for Mother in the now apparently notorious facility living room.

We invited all the staff and residents. Family came from three states, including a 92-year-old relative Mother had not seen in thirty years.

We decorated with banners and balloons and served sandwiches, punch, and a sheet cake that turned out to be delicious. Mother wore a sparkly plastic tiara from the party store and we gave out favors: miniature cars for the men and multicolored Mardi Gras beads for the women.

At the time, I don't think Mother absorbed a bit of it. Mr. X had just come to live in the room next door and she already acted besotted. She was queen for the day and he sat beside her, in the middle of the whole shebang, holding her hand.

One of the staff told my husband that day that Mr. X was *chasing* several women on the unit but we didn't understand the full extent of the euphemism at the time. My cousins and I fretted over where the fickle Mr. X's favor would land and if it were on Mother, whether it would last. We agreed that if having a crush made her happy, then we wished Mr. X a long life and prayed he would not break her heart.

In retrospect, we should have bet on Mother.

As the months passed, apparently she prevailed in the whole high school drama, proving, I guess, that a guy will in fact buy the cow when he is already getting the milk. Or at least that a 90-year-old man will be monogamous if all the other women in his limited field have bashed him about the ankles with their canes or flounced off in a huff, rolling over his steel-arched stability shoes with their walkers.

I think it took Mother a while herself to realize what was going on. Long after the party, whenever I talked to her, she asked me if I knew Mr. X. Then she explained—again—that he lived next door and that they enjoyed each other's company, especially in the evenings after dinner in the living room.

I refrained from saying to her that I had heard about that. Boy howdy, had I heard about that.

Then not too long ago, on another visit, she was showing me the packet of pictures I had sent her after her birthday. I am not sure if she realized that I was the one who had taken them, but that's

81

just the way it is.

"There's Mr. X," she said, pointing him out in the group picture. "I didn't even know I knew him then until I saw these pictures but there he is."

"Yep, there he is," I agreed.

"I guess you could say we're in love," she said.

I guess you could. The two of them don't sit together at meals, though. The tables are assigned by the staff, who have seated them on opposite sides of the dining room. When I join Mother at lunch or dinner sometimes, I can hear his voice. He sings cheerily and tells the same stories over and over again. To tell the truth, they are perfectly suited.

"We have discussed marriage," she said, as I helped her put the pictures away.

I am still trying to get my eyebrows to migrate back down out of my hairline. Who needs Botox when I have my mother to give me a look of perpetual surprise?

The more I think about it, though, the more I doubt I have to worry about planning a wedding.

After all, before Mr. X fell under her spell, he was a chaser. He'll never settle down.

In her heart of hearts, Mother probably likes

it that way.

And I think I now know what "affectionate but not mushy" means.

It means that when it comes to S-E-X, my 91-year-old mother is no talk and all action.

Chapter 9

Hello? I've Lost My Comb

My husband probably has never read John Donne but if he had, Donne would be his favorite seventeenth century English metaphysical poet.

You know his most famous work. *Ask not for whom the bell tolls* . . .

Around our house the most chilling thing you can hear when the phone rings is that it tolls for thee.

With two mothers in their nineties, every call shoots a shiver of fear and speculation down our rapidly hunching spines. Is it one of The Mothers? Which one? Is she all right? What does she need? How many years will it take off my own lifespan to handle it?

Here is how it goes:

We hear the phone. After the second ring, our

talking caller ID kicks in and spits out an incomprehensible audio hairball. *Caw-ull fuh-rom ick-cack-hack.*

It is worst when it is my mother. She lives in a facility with a name totally unpronounceable even by trained human professionals, let alone by a robot.

I am sure the marketers of the place hoped to evoke class, security, and Jane Austen heroines out for a lovely afternoon ramble.

Instead, by the time caller ID coughs it up, the whole thing is just a phonetic hash.

To protect what is left of Mother's privacy, I won't spell it out, but I can tell you without exaggeration the name of the place is two words, seventeen letters long, and consists of vowel pairs heard only in Serbo-Croatian.

Not that I ever need to hear it myself.

Herman is always right on top of the telephone. Even from his distant basement office he will rupture a vocal cord to make sure I know this one's for me.

"It's [Totally Unpronounceable Name]," he yells, with a note of desperation in his cracking voice that begs me to please, oh, please, hurry and pick up so he doesn't have to.

We have an unspoken division of labor about incoming calls. Left to my own devices, I will let them go to voice mail and deal with them on my own timetable.

Herman would rather face the music immediately. If he is home, he answers.

Unless it is Mother.

He gets flustered trying to carry on a phone conversation with her. She cannot hear him, cannot understand his rapid speech and baritone under the best of circumstances, and he is atrocious at the small talk that is about all she can manage anyway these days.

Besides, he knows that he cannot possibly solve the sort of problem that would make her pick up and call. Since her ninety-year-old boyfriend, Mr. X, arrived on the scene, Mother gets plenty of social action right where she lives and hardly ever dials our number just to chat.

These days, Call = Crisis.

Recently, Herman and I came home from dinner out. The message light was blinking. Herman scrolled through caller ID.

"It's from [Totally Unpronounceable Name]," he said, with relief, saved *from* the bell this time.

My gut clenched.

I pressed the play button.

Mother always sounds pitiful on the answering machine, as though she has been kidnapped and is in danger of losing an ear or a finger if I don't rush to her side with ransom.

This night was no different. "Charlotte-Ann?" she said pitifully on the recording. "This is your mother. Charlotte-Ann, I need you to call me, please. I have lost my comb."

By the time I reached her, she already had found it on the floor under the sink and forgotten she had ever called me.

"My comb?" she said, bewildered. "It's in the bathroom. Why?"

Herman and I have talked The Mothers through so many problems on the phone that we could easily get jobs on a tech help desk.

In Mumbai.

It gives me a small level of sympathy for those poor souls who are trying to help harried Americans through the clash of cultures and a mash-up of accents.

The phone rings.

It is Mother.

I pick up the receiver, take a deep breath, and crank up the decibel level while trying to deepen my naturally weedy tone to the bass register she has a chance of processing.

"Mother," I bray like a foghorn. "How are you?"

"Terrible. I am so upset."

"Oh, I'm sorry. What has happened?"

"Someone," she will say dramatically, "Has. Stolen. My. Glasses."

This, of course, is highly unlikely. Her optician has given up on new prescriptions since it is really cataracts that are causing her vision to be so cloudy and nobody in their right mind would try such a delicate operation and recovery on a woman at her age in her mental condition. The glasses in question are bottle-bottom thick trifocals. She has sat on them so many times that both temples stick out at madcap angles and the lenses park askew on her face. She hardly ever uses them anymore but always keeps them in her lap at the ready.

At this point, they are more like a toddler's security blanky or a binky than a tool for vision.

I am sure she *is* upset if they have gone missing.

I use an active listening technique, repeating back to her the last thing she said to me but putting it in the form of a question.

"Someone. Has. Stolen. Your. Glasses?" I ask.

There was a time when after eliciting the details, I would try to tutor her over the phone to speak with one of the staff members and ask them to help her find the missing item.

Now that her hearing has all but disappeared, I just pacify her as much as I can. I tell her she should hang up, wait right there, and I will call her back. I tell her as loudly and as many times as it takes to sink in and when she finally understands and I hear the click of her handset in the cradle, I dial the nurse's station.

They already know what is going on. They always know.

When Mother last lost her glasses, an aide had found them. Tucked in the cushion of my grandmother's favorite chair, the glasses had been swept up inadvertently when the aide had slipped in on the sly and tried to replace Mother's soggy blue plastic disposable underpad with a fresh one. The glasses were—the aide told me—currently soaking in disinfectant. She would have them back in Mother's hands as soon as they were sanitary and dried.

I waited a suitable length of time and called Mother back.

"Well," she said with a tinge of both disgust and triumph in her voice. "The woman who took my glasses has thought better of it and returned them."

Herman has his own struggles with telecommunication. We were watching a movie one night when he remarked, "Have you ever noticed how when someone's on the phone like that you can just fill in the other end of the conversation even though you can't hear it?"

I have indeed.

I spent one of the most entertaining mornings of my life listening to his end of an exchange with his mother, Grannie, about an uncooperative DVD player.

To be precise, I perched on the side of the tub in our bathroom holding my sides and hooting, while he sat on the edge of our bed in his robe and tried to talk her through the emergency.

"Let's look at the remotes," he said. "How many do you have?"

Grannie apparently answered.

He continued.

"Put down the one that says Panasonic."

"No. Put DOWN the one that says Panasonic."

"Can you see that one says Panasonic? You can? Well, put that one down. No. Put it down."

I gathered Grannie was trying to get the player to work so she could show friends the part of a DVD about her hometown in which she appears and speaks to an interviewer. I also gathered that although it was slow going, Herman had finally gotten her to a point where she could see herself on the screen.

"Mom," he said. "Mom."

"MOM. You can watch yourself later. Mom, you can watch that part later. I am trying to tell you how to rewind it to the beginning."

"Mom, I can hear you talking on the DVD. Push pause. Push pause on the remote."

"No. Not the Panasonic remote, the one for the DVD player. No. Put DOWN the one that says Panasonic. Mom, are you listening?"

"I am," I said.

We are still married, although I am afraid one day the bell is going to toll and it is going to be a divorce lawyer. Unless I can get a grip on this uncontrollable laughing.

Chapter 10

I'm the Mother, You're the Child

I always wanted to raise a child. I just never thought she would be 91 years old and my own mother.

The time inevitably has arrived when our roles have reversed.

I know it.

My husband knows it.

The experts all acknowledge it.

The only people who do not seem to get it are our mothers.

After all these years, when things don't go the way they want, both cling to their old fallback position: I'm the mother. You're the child.

It used to work.

The sad thing is, often it still does.

When my father was living, he and Mother

had an extra upstairs room. On the architect's plans for the house, it had been called a sewing room. In reality, besides a small table with a sewing machine and a couple of baskets for thread and notions, the room was overrun with an unholy piled-up jumble of other things with nowhere else to land.

Although he irritated Mother to no end, Daddy called it the lumber room.

I should have known better but I was one of the few people who got a laugh out of my father's wry and contrarian sense of humor: I asked him why.

"Because," he replied, "It's like an old-fashioned hardware store. It has everything in it except lumber."

He could just as easily have called it the kitchen sink.

Herman and I have a lumber room in our basement, plus climate-controlled units at two separate storage places for all the stuff that we haven't felt quite right parting with while The Mothers might still ask for them.

An inventory:

Outdated, undersized clothes that should be

donated to a community theater. Only a character in a play would ever wear them anymore.

Cancelled checks from 25 years ago.

Mounds of faded Kodachrome prints of people who are totally unknown to us and probably completely forgotten by Grannie and Mother, too.

Every Book-of-the-Month Club selection starting somewhere around February 1951 and ending about August 1963.

Bric-a-brac that The Mothers will never use again or miss, but that somehow we cannot bring ourselves to put in a yard sale. Not that it would sell, unless we managed to find a collector of 1950s-era salt and pepper shakers looking for a set with at least one stopper missing and the painted left eye rubbed off either Salty or Peppy, I'm not sure which.

Souvenirs and brochures from cruises and tours of Hawaii, the Mediterranean, London, and Paris.

We didn't take the trips. The Mothers did.

We are afraid to ditch a single thing because they might want or—don't be ridiculous—*need* it someday and we are scared to tell them that as we necessarily helped them downsize, we got rid of it.

After all, it is theirs and they're the Mothers, we're the children.

Except when they behave like children and we have to act *in loco parentis*. That's Latin for *in the place of the parents* but it might as well be what it sounds like: *My mother is making me absolutely loco and every time I look at all this junk, I want to set fire to it, take the insurance money, and move to a spartanly furnished cabin in, oh, I don't know, Idaho?*

Recently, we finally managed to convince Herman's mother to relocate to assisted living. While she was in physical rehab to get her strength back following a hospital stay, he and I sorted all of the belongings in her one-bedroom senior apartment. We stored some, consigned a few others, and moved as much into her studio in the new place as we could cram without being cited by the fire marshal for trapping Grannie under her own debris.

The first day she got there, she was too tired to lodge any protests.

By the morning of Day Two, she wanted to know what had happened to her mirror.

"Here it is," I said, as naive as Bambi in the

headlights, since I had not begun to comprehend where she was going with this.

I was thinking *reflective surface*. She was thinking about the six-foot-long, two-ton horizontal mirror that had formerly been affixed to her dresser.

I held up a decorative gold-framed square number temporarily tucked against the wall in a corner. "Herman can put it up when he comes," I said.

"Not that one," she replied. "That one came from the dollar store."

"Gosh, it's very nice."

Pleased with myself for complimenting her bargain-hunting skills, I hurtled down the path to destruction like a foolish young thing in a *Lifetime Movie Network* Friday night special. If I had been paying attention, I would have heard the entire audience squirm in their seats, thinking *Stop. Look out. Don't go there.*

"I mean," she said, "What happened to *my* mirror?"

Since it was pretty obvious that Grannie's 42-inch 1080-dpi flat screen television (bigger and clearer than anything in our home) was sitting on the dresser, I still was lost. I didn't realize that she thought she could have the TV *and* the mirror, which was so heavy it had required two metal rods and huge screws left over from the Spanish Inquisition to hold it in place. Herman had nearly herniated himself when he struggled it into storage.

"We shouldn't sell it," I had said, as he had looked at it dubiously and, I am sure, wondered if his insides would ever be the same again. "It goes with the bedroom set." The massive bedroom set we had somehow jammed in its entirety into this room where I was now standing ignorant of my impending doom.

Still oblivious, I appraised the wall space in Grannie's new assisted living studio and inspected the back of the bathroom door to see if a full-length mirror would fit.

"What do you want to be able to do?" I now asked her innocently. "Check yourself out from head to toe?"

Grannie snorted. If she had been drinking cola, it would have come out her nose in a froth of derision.

"I want to know what happened to my

mirror."

Light dawned.

"It's in storage," I said, with more cheer than I suddenly felt. "We didn't think it would work with the TV on the dresser."

"What else is in storage?" she wondered, setting a trap that I managed to recognize and evade. *Here, little girl. Don't you want to put your head in this nice warm oven and tell me what you gave to Goodwill without my permission?*

I smiled feebly, the kind of smile that psychologists say is not authentic because it did not reach my suddenly terrified eyes. I stood very still and kept silent.

"At my apartment," Grannie said, "I had that nice, big, long oak stand for the TV."

I knew firsthand what she had for the TV at her apartment. I had scoured the furniture stores, found a good buy, and had it delivered before she ever moved from her old home in the mountains. I managed to keep that point to myself as well as the reminder that at her apartment she had also had a separate bedroom, walk-in closet, and full kitchen. She's the mother. I'm the child.

Or actually, she's Herman's mother. He's her child.

As soon as I got home, I warned Herman what was coming.

The whole situation is something that I think my father would have appreciated. He wasn't much for puns, but oxymorons were right up his alley: those phrases that don't make sense or that make a perfect kind of sense because they contain a contradiction.

Airline food used to be the main example before airlines quit poisoning passengers and decided simply to let them starve for the sake of profits.

Jumbo shrimp.

Herman and I and other caregivers of our ilk are *adult children.*

Exactly.

Those elderly women may be the mothers and we may be the children but someone is going to have to be the adult, and it looks as though we are elected.

"How'd it go with your mother?" I asked Herman the next morning as he and I were lying in bed discussing our plans for the day.

"She wants her mirror," he sighed. "She wants her mirror put back on her dresser and she wants her TV stand."

"You didn't tell her we had consigned the stand, did you?"

"Yeah. I did."

I was surprised he still had his head. Mine would have been sitting on a platter on the dresser or on the gigantic matching chest of drawers. Except that the platter was in storage or maybe in a box in our garage awaiting triage.

"Are you all right?" I asked.

"I think so."

"Was she mad? I guess we could always sell the loveseat instead and get the TV stand back."

"She wants that too," Herman sighed. "I went around the room and asked her piece by piece what she was willing to get rid of. Do you want a bed? Yes. Do you want the dresser? Yes. Do you want the television? Yes."

He gazed mournfully at the ceiling. "It's just like you do with a five-year-old. She finally got the point, I think. So what are you doing today?"

I told him I was working on this chapter. *I'm the mother. You're the child.*

Herman nodded sagely.

"Do you have a story about that?" he asked.

Oh, yes. I think I will tell the one about the mirror.

Chapter 11

Crow with a Side of Blue Cheese Dressing

When I was a journalist in my early thirties, I once got an assignment to fly to Florida and do a magazine feature about a beachfront city's 100th birthday bash.

The hook was that the guests of honor at the Saturday afternoon tea dance and cake cutting would be centenarians and their children. Since the town was known as a retirement destination, it is not surprising that the organizers found a respectably long list of hundred-year-olds and their children to invite.

I am not good at math or demographics under the best of circumstances and my inability to grasp the picture in advance was compounded by my relative youth at the time.

In other words, I was clueless.

Before the event, I anticipated that the party guests would be a nice contingent of elderly gents and ladies like my grandmother; a smattering of folks about my age helping the oldsters with their canes, wheelchairs, and walkers; and a horde of small fry running around in tiny tyke suits and frilly dresses, clutching balloons on curly ribbons: the children.

What a shock when I walked in and everyone was at least seventy years old or better.

I say *better* now that Herman and I are approaching the same stage.

At the time I am quite sure I slapped my forehead and thought *Gad. But of course. They are all ancient.*

I ended up writing a profile of one of the honorees. He had helped to build the Panama Canal as a young man and had met inventor Alexander Graham Bell while he was there. The article took the form of a dialogue with the gentleman's son, who well into his own eighth decade was still suffering the indignity of being known as Junior.

The two argued through the entire interview, about the father's cigar smoking and whiskey drinking, about whether Dad should be so flirtatious with a reporter, and about how many men had orbited the moon, among other things.

It was hilarious to me at the time.

Now I realize that Junior probably went home and ate an entire carton of snack cakes in one sitting before falling dog-tired into bed.

I wish I had remembered that encounter years ago when Herman and I first waded into the thick of all this eldercare. I also might have remembered to keep my sense of humor.

It is not easy.

It is never easy.

It is not easy to grow old. It must be particularly hard to be gracious about your daily decline, losses, and failings.

It is hard to be the last member of your own birth family.

It is hard to watch your children give away your treasured things in order to move you into smaller and smaller quarters.

It is hard to give up control of the life that once belonged to you.

It is not easy to accompany someone through

old age, either. It is rarely convenient, often exasperating, even infuriating, and sometimes it will make you cry and break your heart.

Can I get a witness?

So many women—and some men—of my acquaintance are on the journey with elderly parents right now.

I know a woman with one child in high school and another in college. Along with her brother and two sisters, they share the caregiving for their widowed mother. Now that their mom can no longer stay by herself on the family farm, even in the warm months of spring and fall, the four siblings move her around among their own homes.

It is upsetting for an oldster not to be settled somewhere and the grown children are not equally equipped emotionally to deal with the toll of constantly having an anxious, fragile presence in the house. My friend bears the brunt, I think, because she seems the least bowled over by it all.

"It is what it is," she says and shrugs.

When I was at my most resentful of my own situation sometimes I wanted to slap my friend like Cher popped Nicolas Cage in *Moonstruck*.

Snap out of it, I wanted to say. *You are making me look hopelessly melodramatic. Can you really be that stoic?*

Now I believe I should have heard her silent cry for empathy and baked a couple of dozen brownies for us to share.

I also know a pair of sisters who rarely agree on what is best for their mother. I am close to the younger one and we get on the phone occasionally to bond over our troubles. I carp about the outlandish things The Mothers have done. She grumbles about her sister. As difficult as it is to be the only child, as I am, sometimes I thank my lucky stars. The only knock-down drag-outs I get into are with my own conscience and ill-humor.

Another friend moved to be near her children, her grandchildren, and activities she loves with the intention of enjoying her own retirement. Instead, three or four times a week, she finds herself driving a hundred miles roundtrip through awful urban traffic at the beck and call of her own addled, frail, but stubborn parents.

Every time I ask her how they are doing, she starts to rant.

I don't mind. It is fine to let it out around me. I have been there.

On the Sunday morning that Grannie sat down on the sofa and could not get up, I am going to tell you the truth: I was totally fed up and not ashamed to say so to anyone who would listen without gasping at my scandalous lack of sensitivity.

When I started writing this book, I was writing it for myself. For catharsis.

I looked it up. It means a purge of pent-up emotions and socially unacceptable feelings.

It must have worked because somewhere between the first chapter and the last, I started thinking this stuff truly *is* funny.

What's not to love about a mother whose short term memory is so bad she forgets that blue cheesy stuff is supposed to be salad dressing and starts gobbling it by the spoonful? I have wanted to do that myself.

Okay, fine. Maybe I have even sneaked the bottle out of the refrigerator door and snacked on it once or twice.

I told you I have had my moments.

And now, I am going to have to eat my salad

dressing and cookies with a whole lot of crow, because after years of The Mothers driving me crazy, I am forced to a not-so-painful admission.

As it turns out, Grannie was right when she called me from the sofa so early on that Sunday morning.

It took her years to finally do it, but at least she made me laugh.

Acknowledgments

Never did I imagine that I would finish a book. I have always claimed to be a sprinter, not built for a marathon. Without the gift of friends, family, and colleagues who goosed me into starting, encouraged me to persevere, and have cheered me on as I have tied up all the many loose ends necessary to publish, I would not have made it. Thank you Kipling, Marland, Carmen, Thomas, Mary Ann, Marion, Beth, Charlie, Meredith, Jason, Heather, Agnes, Jacqueline, Karen, Lattreta, Margrit, Ruth, and Nancy for listening, for laughing, and for egging me on. You are deeply appreciated.

Every woman who writes should be blessed with a husband like Herman. He is unfailingly supportive and enthusiastic, an endless source of material, a willing foil in my stories, and the love of my life. Sweetheart, I adore you.

Jami and Kevin helped me more than they will ever know with their thorough reading of the manuscript and their forthright assessments. I count it one of my greatest joys to have friends I can trust to be thoughtful and honest when I need it most.

Tammie's belief in me has been unshakeable and her example has urged me forward. How she finds thirty-six hours in every day and the strength to dodge all the curveballs that those days throw at her, I will never know.

I am so lucky to have discovered Vera Pastore, an editor with spirit, candor, a robust laugh, and a love of precision. Any mistakes at this point are surely my own.

I thank Neva for introducing me to Maria Christina Schultz, whose ability to visually translate my half-baked ideas into an appetite-whetting cover has amazed me.

Finally, I must thank The Mothers, who had no idea when they spawned us that they would wind up as the muses and subjects of such a frank and, I hope, funny book. To them, I owe my senses of humor and of outrage . . . but certainly not of propriety. I pray that they will forgive me my sins.

About the Author

Charlotte Johnson Jones lives in Fredericksburg, Virginia, where she recently retired from a second career as reference and social sciences librarian at a small liberal arts university.

In the 1980s and 1990s, under the byline C. J. Houtchens, she wrote for many national publications, including *The Washington Post, Travel and Leisure, Harper's Bazaar,* and *USA Weekend,* and profiled such diverse personalities as Maya Angelou, Sissy Spacek, two Miss America winners, African princess Elizabeth of Toro, musicians, artists, political appointees, and the panda keeper at the National Zoo.

When not consumed by coping with their elders, Jones and her husband, Herman, travel the United States in a motor home, squandering his grown children's inheritance and having a fine time. Their escapades are the subject of Jones's next book, tentatively titled *Forty Feet Long and Eight Miles per Gallon.* Or maybe *Just Keep Driving Darling, We Can Always Get Divorced in Reno.*

Made in the USA
Lexington, KY
30 September 2012